The Rabbi and the Reverend

For Howard and Rocky —A.A.
To my best friends: Marina, Carla, Riccardo, Mauro —C.F.

KAR-BEN PUBLISHING®
An imprint of Lerner Publishing Group, Inc.
241 First Avenue North
Minneapolis, MN 55401 USA

Website address: www.karben.com

Photo credit: Arnie Sachs/CNP/MediaPunch/Alamy Stock Photo, p. 29.

Main body text set in Adobe Caslon Pro.
Typeface provided by Adobe Systems.

Library of Congress Cataloging-in-Publication Data

Names: Ades, Audrey, author. | Fedele, Chiara, illustrator.
Title: The rabbi and the reverend : Joachim Prinz, Martin Luther King Jr., and their fight against silence / by Audrey Ades ; illustrated by Chiara Fedele.
Description: Minnepolis, MN : Kar-Ben Publishing, An imprint of Lerner Publishing Group, Inc., [2021] | Includes bibliographical references. | Audience: Ages 4–10 | Audience: Grades 2–3 | Summary: "This is the story of two men, Dr. Martin Luther King, Jr., and Rabbi Joachim Prinz, an immigrant from Nazi Germany, with a shared belief that remaining silent in the face of injustice was wrong" —Provided by publisher.
Identifiers: LCCN 2020040471 (print) | LCCN 2020040472 (ebook) | ISBN 9781541589766 | ISBN 9781541589773 (paperback) | ISBN 9781728428956 (ebook)
Subjects: LCSH: King, Martin Luther, Jr., 1929–1968—Friends and associates—Juvenile literature. | Prinz, Joachim, 1902–1988—Friends and associates—Juvenile literature. | African American clergy—Biography—Juvenile literature. | African American civil rights workers—Biography—Juvenile literature. | Rabbis—United States—Biography—Juvenile literature. | African Americans—Civil rights—History—20th century—Juvenile literature. | Civil rights movements—United States—History—20th century—Juvenile literature. | United States—Politics and government—1961–1963—Juvenile literature.
Classification: LCC E185.97.K5 R28 2021 (print) | LCC E185.97.K5 (ebook) | DDC 323.092/2 [B]—dc23

LC record available at https://lccn.loc.gov/2020040471
LC ebook record available at https://lccn.loc.gov/2020040472

Manufactured in the United States of America
1-47486-48031-1/19/2021

The Rabbi and the Reverend

Joachim Prinz, Martin Luther King Jr., and Their Fight against Silence

Audrey Ades

illustrated by Chiara Fedele

KAR-BEN
PUBLISHING

Oppeln, Germany: 1910

Before the sun came up, Joachim trudged through the snow to Rabbi Goldmann's house.

"Climb up here," said the rabbi. "I need your help."

Joachim squeezed between the bundles of food and clothing piled high behind the driver's seat.

As the horse clip-clopped through the cobblestone streets, Joachim helped the rabbi drop packages at the doorsteps of families who needed extra help to make it through the winter.

With each package he delivered, Joachim felt like he was making a little difference in the world.

When he grew up, Joachim Prinz studied Torah and became a rabbi, just like Rabbi Goldmann.

Rabbi Prinz gave powerful sermons, and he wasn't afraid to speak up when he saw wrongdoing.

By 1933, Adolf Hitler had taken control of the German government. Hitler hated the Jewish people. He blamed them for Germany's problems. He took away their businesses and their right to vote. He forced them from their homes and made their children leave school.

Most Germans pretended not to notice what was happening. Speaking up against these injustices could get a person into trouble. Joachim believed his neighbors' silence was as bad as Hitler's laws.

Joachim gave sermons about freedom and equal rights. He begged Jews to leave Germany. Joachim's words were against the law. The police arrested him so many times that he was no longer surprised to see them at the back of his synagogue.

In 1937, the German police ordered the
rabbi and his family to leave Germany.

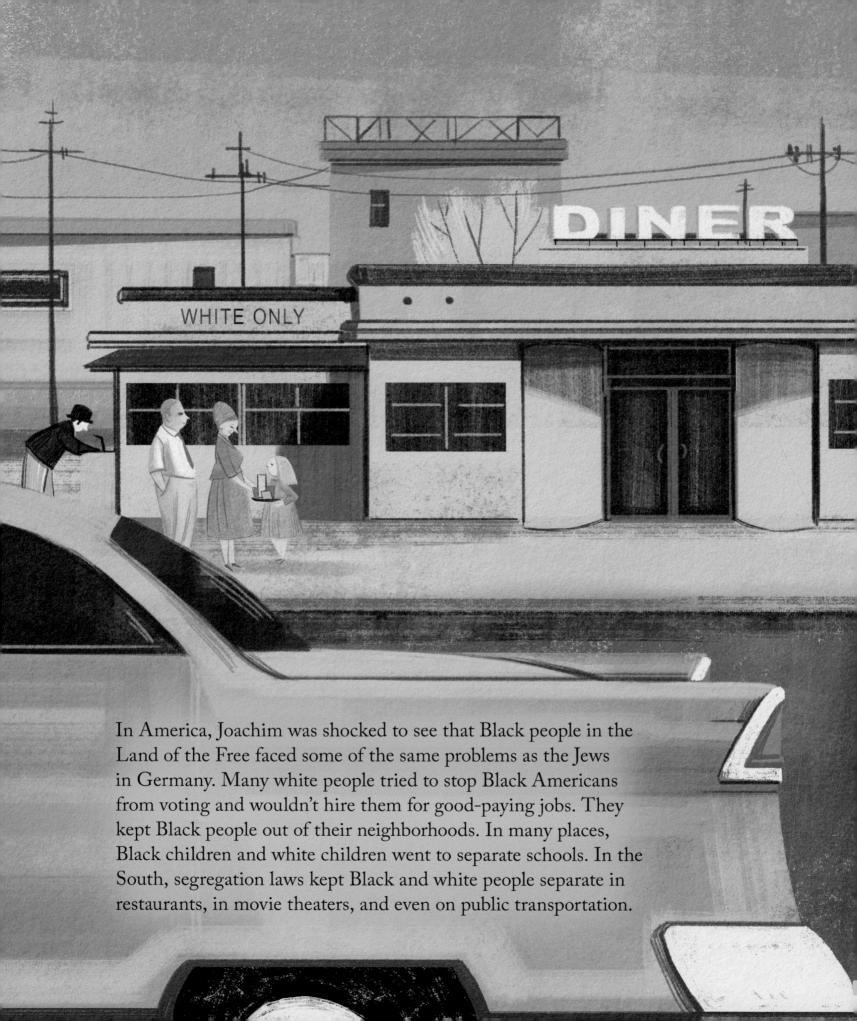

In America, Joachim was shocked to see that Black people in the Land of the Free faced some of the same problems as the Jews in Germany. Many white people tried to stop Black Americans from voting and wouldn't hire them for good-paying jobs. They kept Black people out of their neighborhoods. In many places, Black children and white children went to separate schools. In the South, segregation laws kept Black and white people separate in restaurants, in movie theaters, and even on public transportation.

Joachim spoke out about these injustices to anyone who would listen. In Germany, he had seen what could happen when people stood by while their neighbors suffered. Why didn't more people speak up when they saw others treated unfairly?

He wasn't the only one asking this question.

COLORED ONLY

Atlanta, Georgia: 1935

Six-year-old Martin King walked to school by himself. His best buddy had to go to a different school because his skin was a different color than Martin's. This didn't seem right. How could the grown-ups allow this to happen?

As he grew up, Martin noticed that the color of a person's skin mattered a lot. White kids got new books. They got seats at the front of the bus, tables at restaurants, and houses in the pretty parts of town. Black kids did not.

Martin studied the Bible and became a minister. In his church, the congregation responded with a big "Amen" when the Reverend King encouraged them to speak out against injustice. But outside the church walls, that kind of talk could get a person into trouble.

Montgomery, Alabama: 1955

Martin wasn't afraid of trouble. In the southern city of Montgomery, Black people were tired of boarding buses through the rear door and sitting at the back. Martin helped lead a peaceful protest against the bus company. For a whole year, Black citizens of Montgomery walked wherever they needed to go. The bus company lost so much money that it changed its rules so Black riders could sit where they pleased.

Joachim read about the minister from Georgia who demanded equal rights for his people.

Martin heard about the rabbi from Germany who raised his voice for justice.

Their shared message connected them. They gave each other support and advice in the fight for civil rights.

Martin spoke at Joachim's synagogue in New Jersey.

Joachim sent words of courage and hope
when Martin was jailed.

Joined by thousands of people who would not stay silent, the rabbi and the reverend participated in pickets and protests demanding fair treatment for all Americans. They knew that until people spoke up for the rights of others, the country would never be truly free.

Washington, DC: August 28, 1963

Martin and Joachim stood together on the National Mall, facing the Washington Monument. They were leaders of the March on Washington, the largest civil rights gathering the country had ever seen. Thousands of people stood shoulder to shoulder. Millions more watched on television or listened on their radios.

The crowd hushed as Joachim stepped up to the microphone.

"When I was the rabbi of the Jewish community in Berlin under the Hitler regime, I learned many things," he said. "The most important thing that I learned . . . was that bigotry and hatred are not the most urgent problems. The most urgent, the most disgraceful, the most shameful and the most tragic problem is silence. America must not remain silent."

Then it was Martin's turn.

"I have a dream that one day this nation will rise up and live out the true meaning of its creed, 'We hold these truths to be self-evident, that all men are created equal.'"

Martin's voice was strong and clear. "And when this happens, when we allow freedom to ring . . . all of God's children, black men and white men, Jews and Gentiles, Protestants and Catholics, will be able to join hands and sing in the words of the old Negro spiritual, 'Free at last! Free at last! Thank God Almighty, we are free at last!'"

After they finished speaking, President John F. Kennedy invited Martin, Joachim, and the other leaders of the march to the White House. The president promised to push harder for laws that would protect the rights of Black citizens.

Martin and Joachim knew the president would do his best. But he couldn't do it alone. Every American had to speak up for equality and freedom. No one could remain silent until there was justice for all.

Timeline

1902   Joachim Prinz is born in the tiny town of Burkhardtsdorf, Germany.

1910   The Prinz family moves to Oppeln, a bigger town with more Jews and better schools.

1926   Joachim Prinz becomes the youngest rabbi in Germany at the age of twenty-four.

1929   Martin Luther King Jr. is born in Atlanta, Georgia. His father is the pastor of Ebenezer Baptist Church.

1933   Under the rule of Adolf Hitler and the Nazi Party, Jews in Germany lose many of their rights. Joachim warns his fellow Jews to leave the country.

1937   Joachim leaves Germany and comes to America.

1954   While still completing his Ph.D., Martin becomes pastor of the Dexter Avenue Baptist Church in Montgomery, Alabama.

1955   Martin leads the Montgomery Bus Boycott in Montgomery, Alabama. It is the first of many peaceful boycotts, sit-ins, and demonstrations he helps to organize and support.

1958   Joachim becomes president of the American Jewish Congress, an organization that supports the civil rights movement. He meets Martin Luther King Jr.

1962   Joachim invites Martin to speak at his synagogue in Newark, New Jersey. Two thousand people showed up to hear him speak.

1963   Martin and Joachim are two of the ten key speakers at the March on Washington for Jobs and Freedom in Washington, DC, on August 28.

1963 President John F. Kennedy is assassinated on November 22.

1964 President Lyndon B. Johnson signs the Civil Rights Act. This law bans discrimination based on race, color, religion, sex, or national origin. It outlaws unfair voter registration requirements, separate schools for Black and white children, employment discrimination, and separate areas for Black and white people in public spaces.

1965 Some states and counties find ways to keep Black Americans from voting even though the Civil Rights Act prohibits it. Johnson signs the Voting Rights Act of 1965 to make it harder to deprive Black people of their right to vote.

1968 Martin Luther King Jr. is assassinated on April 4 in Memphis, Tennessee. Joachim attends the funeral. Joachim participates in a protest march in Martin's memory in Memphis on April 8.

1988 Joachim Prinz dies in Livingston, New Jersey.

Dr. Martin Luther King Jr. and Rabbi Joachim Prinz at the March on Washington for Jobs and Freedom in Washington, DC, August 28, 1963.

Glossary

bigotry: intolerance of a group, race, religion, or belief that is not your own

boycott: to refuse to buy, use, or participate as a form of protest

civil rights: the rights that every person should have regardless of their sex, race, or religion

creed: a set of guiding beliefs held by an individual or a group

Negro: a term for Black people that was common for much of the twentieth century. It was not considered disrespectful during the civil rights era but is now often considered offensive.

picket: to stand or walk in front of a business or building to protest or demand something

regime: a ruling government

segregation: the separation of one group of people—usually one racial group—from another

Further Reading

Churnin, Nancy. *Martin & Anne: The Kindred Spirits of Dr. Martin Luther King, Jr. and Anne Frank.* Berkeley, CA: Creston Books, 2019.

Kelley, Kitty. *Martin's Dream Day.* New York: Atheneum Books for Young Readers, 2017.

Michelson, Richard. *As Good as Anybody: Martin Luther King, Jr. and Abraham Joshua Heschel's Amazing March toward Freedom.* New York: Alfred A. Knopf, 2008.

Pinkney, Andrea Davis, and Brian Pinkney. *Martin & Mahalia: His Words, Her Song.* New York: Little Brown, 2013.

Swain, Gwenyth. *Riding to Washington.* Chelsea, MI: Sleeping Bear, 2008.

Author's Acknowledgment

I would like to thank Rabbi Jonathan Prinz, Rachel Eskin Fisher, Rachel Nierenberg Pasternak, and the American Jewish Archives for their generous contributions of time and information for this book.

The speeches of Rabbi Prinz and the Reverend King have been shortened for this book. You can read their full speeches online.

About the Author

Audrey Ades grew up in New England and holds degrees in theater and psychology. Her previous picture books include *Judah Touro Didn't Want to be Famous*. She lives in South Florida with her husband, son, and persnickety Pomeranian, Cookie.

About the Illustrator

Chiara Fedele was born in Milan, Italy. After graduating from art school, she attended the Brera Academy in Milan. Her illustrations have appeared in many picture books, including *Yaffa and Fatima: Shalom, Salaam*. She also teaches drawing and painting techniques. She lives in Pavia, Italy.